Encouraging Your Heart
15 Ways to See, Hear, and Know God Better

Donnella Cranford

Expert Publishing, Inc.
Andover, Minnesota

All scripture quotations are taken from the New King James
Version (NKJV), Thomas Nelson Publishers, Nashville. Thomas
Nelson Publishers, Copyright 1982. Used by permission. All rights
reserved.

ISBN 10: 1-931945-91-8
ISBN 13: 978-1-931945-91-2

Library of Congress Catalog Number: 2008936417

Printed in the United States of America

First Printing: September 2008

12 11 10 09 08   5 4 3 2 1

Andover,
Minnesota

Expert Publishing, Inc.
14314 Thrush Street NW,
Andover, MN 55304-3330
1-877-755-4966
www.expertpublishinginc.com

Dedication

This book is dedicated

with love and appreciation

to my mother,

Maude Devella Brown,

who has given me life

and throughout it has constantly

supported, directed, and encouraged

my journey.

From My Heart to Yours, Mom

FROM GOD'S HEART TO YOURS

What Others Have To Say About Encouraging Your Heart

There is power in every word through out this dynamic book. Donnella has done an outstanding job by allowing the power of the Holy Spirit to guide her in this endeavor. You will undoubtedly be blessed beyond measure as you experience this same power throughout these written pages. Your life will be forever changed.

--Roz Tandy, Training Director of The LUKE Agency, Author of Discovering My Greatness & Customer Service in God's House

Donnella Cranford has written the most positive must-read guidebook on living a holy life. She gives practical advice for making choices and facing challenges. And she does it all without being preachy.

--Emily Semien, wife and mother

It is a state of sheer bliss to see, hear, and know Jesus Christ. Donnella Cranford has given us a blueprint for establishing a more personal relationship with God. This is certainly a book I will share with the ones I love. The information in this book will assist any reader in ascertaining or reclaiming their eternal union with the Most High God.

--Tennille White, President of Tennille White Chicago, Inc.

Donnella's life embodies James 1:22. She consistently and deliberately chooses to do what the word says, making her credible in encouraging others to do the same. Reading *Encouraging Your Heart* is like having a conversation with Donnella. After having many encouraging conversations with her myself, I have grown as a Christian, and enjoy a deeper relationship with Christ because of her guidance and living witness. Readers of *Encouraging Your Heart* will experience the same blessings.

--Juliana Mimms, President of The Education Firm, LLC

Donnella Cranford continues in the great legacy of the One who has shown us the way to a full and fulfilling life in the richness of relationship with God. Instead of looking to outside remedies, her words of encouragement remind us that we need only welcome and embrace the inside relationship we are privileged to have with our Heavenly Father to experience the abundant life promised by Jesus Christ. This is a wonderful book that is a must read for all who love the Lord.

--Dr. Belinda Johnson White, Associate Professor at Morehouse College and Author of Dr. White's 21st Century Guide to Leadership and Professional Development

FROM GOD'S HEART TO YOURS

And do not be conformed to this world, but be transformed by the renewing of your mind, that you may prove what is that good and acceptable and perfect will of God.

Romans 12:2

FROM GOD'S HEART TO YOURS

Contents

FROM GOD'S HEART TO YOURS

Foreword

A s women, we walk a special path upon this earth. We nurture life, build community, search for meaning, and impart life lessons to others. Often in our caretaking roles, we forget that the most important trip we must take is the journey inward to discover ourselves.

Through her inspired words of wisdom, Minister Donnella Cranford encourages us to walk in God's footsteps and to see ourselves reflected in His beautiful image. She reminds us to step aside from the worldly definitions of successes and the expectations of others. Only then we can come to know our true selves—not as others would have us be, but as women after God's own heart.

God is working through Donnella Cranford in a powerful way. This is a book that changes lives. Each ENCOURAGEMENT takes you to a higher level of knowing God's will and God's way for us. Journey through these pages with eyes and hearts wide open, and you will be blessed by endless gems of Truth.

> --Dr. Delorese Ambrose, international speaker, author of *Leadership—The Journey Inward* and *Making Peace with Your Work*

FROM GOD'S HEART TO YOURS

A Letter to My Sisters

My Sister:

*D*o you search to find yourself only to be frustrated as you attempt to become whatever the present day image of a beautiful woman is? Do you seek security and purpose from worldly sources—personal success, status, beauty, wealth, and the approval of others? To meet these needs, we drive ourselves to achieve, to please, and to spend endless hours and dollars trying to look a certain way, be a certain way, and act a certain way. I know because I have been there and continue to strive to stay away from there.

This book is a collection of messages I have prepared and taught over the years that have transformed my life and renewed my mind. They have impacted and encouraged my life and the lives of others; let them make a difference in your life.

God's desire is for us to come into the knowledge and understanding of knowing who we truly are in Him. We are women after God's own heart because according to Genesis 1:27, we are designed by Him and made in His image and likeness. Because we have accepted Christ as our personal Savior, we have the opportunity to become new creatures in Him as we strive to mirror the character of Christ. That is what I have done and continue to do as the Father allows me to remain on this side of heaven.

My sister, we do not have to pretend to be someone other than who God has made us to be. And that means we have to know the truth because the truth is what sets us free according to John 8:32, 8:36.

Paul wrote in Romans 12:2 that our lives are to be transformed by the renewing of our minds. I pray that your life will be transformed, your mind renewed, and your spirit encouraged as you read the messages between the covers of this book from my heart to yours, in Jesus' name. Let's begin this journey and allow the Holy Spirit to minister to your heart from mine.

Always in His Love,

Donnetta

FROM GOD'S HEART TO YOURS

Acknowledgements

$\mathcal{O}$ ver the years, many have encouraged me to write a book, but it was not until the Saturday morning of September 15, 2007, at 7:45 am, when the Lord directed Rolawn Evans to instruct me to get the first book written and published. It was at that point that I moved on the leading of the Holy Spirit. Rolawn, I will forever be grateful to you.

Many have been a part of making this dream come true, and it would be impossible to name each person. So, I say a universal thank you to everyone. I am eternally grateful to Dr. Delorese Ambrose, who was sent as my book angel at a most critical time in the final stages of my completing this book; God knew what I needed and sent me you. And, to Mary Jane Holt, who gave the book the first critical eye, thank you for being you.

Without praying and fasting, this book would not be in your hands, so to Annette Miles, who has been my prayer partner for over fifteen years and to Joan Cranford, who is my every Wednesday fasting partner, God used you in a mighty way, and for that I am appreciative. A special thanks to Tennille White, my goddaughter who championed my efforts and prayed for me and with me throughout the process.

Of course, I must praise God and give thanks for Reggie Tolbert, who designed the cover and layout of this book and spent many hours working closely with me and the wonderful people at Expert Publishing, Inc.

Most of all, I thank my family for your untiring support, encouragement, and patience. Patricia

Acknowledgements

Everette, my sister, consistently advised me to be sure and get the necessary rest I needed so I could refocus, and allow God to reveal His direction to me for this book. To my husband, Haywood, who provided the love that moves mountains and my son, Paul, who motivated me to push forward by modeling the way and completing his first script, I am lovingly grateful to you both for sharing my life.

--DBC

FROM GOD'S HEART TO YOURS

Introduction
Show Off Your Birthmark

*M*any people are born with a birthmark, a visible sign that is on the body from birth. When we become Christians, we are born again and, in that second birth, we are born with a birthmark, a visible sign of the character of Christ.

After the second birth, our life is radically and immediately reoriented to reflect the character of Christ. We submit to Christ and our lives are transformed. The transformation is an inside job that is reflected in our outward behavior. God's desire for our lives involves inner qualities as well as outward behavior. Now that we live for Christ instead of ourselves, it is God who works in us to will and to act according to His good purpose (Philippians 2:13). God will make Himself real to you if you seek Him.

We walk in the light because God is light (I John 1:5). The truth is, we are to reflect the light that is the character of Christ. In the light, nothing is hidden. In the light, there is honesty, integrity, and purity (1 John 3:3). There is consistency between what is inside and what is outside, between belief and behavior, between our words and our ways, between our attitude and our actions, between our values and our practice.

As a little girl, I believed Christ was my personal Savior, that He had died for me, and that He was the Son of God. What was missing was the personal relationship with Christ that came only from me seeking Him out and getting to know Him better. I had to study His Word, pray, and reach out to the Lord so that a relationship was developed.

1

The transformation I experienced has changed my life tremendously. I love my life and who God created me to be, and I want you to experience this same transformation—a closer, more personal relationship with Christ—and see your life move from glory to glory to glory as your heart is encouraged. Grow your personal relationship with the Lord, for He is waiting to speak directly to your heart.

All of us who are baptized into Christ's family have clothed ourselves with Christ (Galatians 3:27); this is done through the second birth, so walk in the light and show off your birthmark from your second birth!

FROM GOD'S HEART TO YOURS

How to Use this Book

*B*egin by asking God to give you wisdom, clear insight, revelation knowledge, and the understanding of how to apply each Encouragement to your personal life. I recommend that you read one Encouragement at a time, meditate on the scripture listed in From God's Heart to Yours, and write your Reflections as the Holy Spirit ministers to you. Always remember:

Eye has not seen, nor ear heard,
Nor have entered into the heart of man
The things which God has prepared for those
who love Him.
I Corinthians 2:9

I have found that journaling my thoughts allows me to have a reference to what I received at that given moment. It serves as a means to measure growth and as a witness to prayers being answered. God is all knowing and all powerful and will provide you awareness beyond the mind of the natural man.

The journey through this book is all personal and the experience can be as great as you want, based on what you put into it. I am only making a recommendation; you might find your own method of using this book. This journey is a personal relationship between you and our Lord and Savior. Just allow the Spirit of the living God to work in and through you to be encouraged and move you from glory to glory to glory.

Encouragement One

Walk in the Beauty of Holiness: It's a Choice

Encouragement One

Walk in the Beauty of Holiness: It's a Choice

*W*e are given so many choices on this journey called life: the choice to say whatever we want, whenever we want; the choice to worship any way we want and wherever we want; and choices of many foods, clothing, and shelter—just to name a few. Every decision involves choices.

I Chronicles 16:29 tells us we are to give to the Lord the glory due His name and to worship Him in the beauty of holiness! We are created for God's glory, to worship Him in spirit and in truth, and one way of worshiping and giving the Lord glory is to walk in the beauty of holiness.

Holiness, to me, is that quality of life evidenced by godliness, purity, and consecration to God. I'd like to give you a one word definition for holiness—holiness is Christ-like. Being holy is to be more like Jesus Christ.

The Bible teaches us that we have one of two lifestyles—either a lifestyle in the flesh or a lifestyle in the Spirit. We either choose to live according to our natural impulses and desires, making decisions and choices solely on the basis of what pleases us personally, or

7

we can choose to live according to actions that the Holy Spirit authorizes and compels us to take.

The desires of the flesh repulse the Spirit, and the desires of the Spirit repulse the flesh. Either way, one thing remains constant—walking in the beauty of holiness is your choice.

Check yourself out; take the following holiness test. You don't have to say OUCH, but you know in your heart what the answer is. Has this ever happened to you?

- I don't have any cash on me, but I sure would like something from the office coffee bar. No one will miss one cup of coffee. After all, everyone else in the office does it.
- I don't need to report all my income on my taxes. After all, Uncle Sam sticks it to me all year; this one's for me.
- Should I give my tithe or go and purchase the new dress I saw on sale?
- You are in a group setting and your friends are talking about a certain family in the neighborhood. One of the family members shared something with you in confidence and sharing it could really devastate your trusted relationship. But sharing it with your friends really could spice up the conversation.

Our flesh wants to do what comes natural, to be self-seeking and self-satisfying. We have to exchange self-like conduct (doing what we want) for Christ-like conduct, characterized by a Spirit-led life and evidenced by a woman walking in the beauty of holiness, and that means mirroring the character of Christ. You make this decision deliberately, and only you can make it.

In Galatians, the scriptures outline the self-seeking character as works of the flesh and the Christ-like character as fruit of the Spirit. What leaps out at me is the contrast between the types of things that are listed as being the fruit of the Spirit and those that are listed as works of the flesh. The works of the flesh are described as acts of the sinful nature and they are just that—actions, things we do. The fruit of the Spirit, on the other hand, are character traits. They are ways of being, and they will manifest themselves in behaviors consistent with the life of the Spirit.

We cannot walk in the beauty of holiness without assistance. Holiness is Christ's character produced in us by the Holy Spirit as a result of our yielding to His working in our lives. Draw near to God and He will draw near to you (James 4:8). It is your choice.

In I Peter 1:15-16, Peter admonishes us to be holy in our conduct because Christ is holy. To be holy is to be set apart—set apart from sin and impurities, to act and speak differently than the world.

In receiving Christ, we choose to receive His character: kindness, faithfulness, gentleness, self-control, love, joy, peace, longsuffering—the Fruit of the Spirit. How well are you doing? As we walk in the beauty of holiness, we have willingly decided that the Spirit of God will be our guide. The essential question I use is: what would I do or say if Jesus was sitting or standing directly next to me—right now?

We cannot shuck and jive:
- Ask the woman with the alabaster box who washed the feet of Jesus with her hair and expensive perfume—called to walk in the beauty of holiness.

9

• Ask Mary Magdalene, a woman characterized as a prostitute, who possessed seven demons—called to walk in the beauty of holiness.

• Ask Deborah, a judge called to walk in the beauty of holiness, who sat daily and listened to the people—called to walk in the beauty of holiness.

• Ask the woman at the well, who decided to drink the water of life—called to walk in the beauty of holiness.

• Or ask Esther, a woman in a position to save a nation—called to walk in the beauty of holiness.

All of them had a choice and they each chose to walk in the beauty of holiness. You, too, have a choice: allow the flesh to control you, which will lead to death and destruction, or you can choose this day to allow the Holy Spirit to lead and control you, which will produce a bountiful harvest of joy everlasting in your life as you walk in the beauty of holiness.

Today, what choice will you make to be more in alignment with the beauty of holiness?

FROM GOD'S HEART TO YOURS

1 Chronicles 16:29

From Your Heart to God's
REFLECTIONS

Encouragement Two

Check your Mind, Mood, and Attitude

Encouragement Two

Check your Mind, Mood, and Attitude

*A*re you examining your mind, mood, and attitude regularly to see if you are mirroring the character of Christ? The three of them work together to reflect who we are. I ask that question because so often we don't realize the impact we have on others. Our mind, mood, and attitude not only affect us personally; they also have an effect on the people we are around.

Have you ever awakened in the morning and not felt like getting up and going to school or to work? Sure, we all have. If you did not change your thinking immediately, your family, friends, and others you'd come in contact with would be affected. It could even result in you and others having a bad day because of your negative attitude. Ask me, because I have been there.

Our attitude is the first thing people see. Our mood is shown in our attitude, and they both are the result of what is going on in our mind. We talk about other people and their attitudes, especially their negative attitudes, but have you checked yours lately—your mind, mood, and attitude?

To be sure we are on the same page, here is my definition of attitude. It is our disposition, our outward expression of our inward thoughts. An attitude can be negative or positive. And, because it is our goal to be more like Jesus, our attitude should always be positive. That is why it is so critical to constantly work on building our personal relationship with Christ. Even when we don't feel like being positive, we must be positive anyway for Christ's sake. Remember, we are a reflection of the character of Christ.

We have control over our mind, mood, and attitude. It all starts with our thoughts. Too often our thoughts are influenced by worldly values. We allow outside influences to affect our thinking. Romans 12:2 tells us we are not to be conformed to this world, but transformed by the renewing of our mind.

In order for our outer life to be reflective of Christ, we have to be renewed within. We have to be aware of what thoughts go into our minds and what actions we display. We are transformed from the inside out, not from the outside in. Always remember that your character is reflected in your actions.

Our outer life is our reputation with people. And we want our reputation to be good because we are to reflect Christ wherever we go, in whatever we do, and in whatever we say. What kind of reputation do you have?

Be deliberate in reflecting the attitude of Christ. The best place to start is at the Sermon on the Mount, with the Beatitudes. Take a close look at Matthew 5:3-12. There is a series of statements that start off with the words BLESSED ARE. Blessed simply means empowered to flourish. That's what we want to reflect in our mind, mood, and attitude.

Jesus gives us a set of attitudes that will empower us to flourish in various ways. Put BLESSED AM I in your mind as you reflect on these verses of scripture. Then, watch your mind, mood, and attitude become more like what Christ would have them to be.

- Blessed are the poor in spirit—the poor in spirit are those who recognize their spiritual poverty and cast aside all self-dependency.
- Blessed are those who mourn—those who mourn are not necessarily those in bereavement, but those who experience the sorrow of repentance for doing something wrong.
- Blessed are the meek—those who are meek are not weak, but rather have controlled strength in God's promises.
- Blessed are the ones who hunger and thirst for righteousness—those who hunger and thirst for righteousness will search the Bible for answers to their situations, instead of searching out people.
- Blessed are the merciful—those who are merciful practice the principle of reaping and sowing.
- Blessed are the pure in heart—those who are pure in heart have pure motives; they examine their life by God's standard. Check your motives.
- Blessed are the peacemakers—the opposite of a troublemaker is a peacemaker. Those who are peacemakers don't get involved in stirring up strife, discord, or confusion among the brethren. Be a peacemaker.
- Blessed are those who are persecuted for righteousness' sake—for those who are persecuted for righteousness' sake, the Bible tells us, the kingdom of heaven is theirs.

17

It's time for a mind, mood, and attitude check-up; do it today. Check your attitude by the Beatitude and live a life that is reflective of the character of Christ.

Which Beatitude reminds you of a mind, mood, or attitude shift you need to make today?

From Your Heart to God's
REFLECTIONS

Encouragement Three
Know That You are Designed By God
(So You Must Be BEAUTIFUL and the Best)

Encouragement Three

Know That You are Designed By God (So You Must Be BEAUTIFUL and the Best)

*S*ociety's images of women shift as quickly as fashion trends. Many women spend a lifetime searching to find where they fit, only to be deceived or frustrated as they attempt to become whatever the present day image of a beautiful woman is. We are fascinated with beauty. The beauty industry is one of the largest in the world. We spend vast amounts of money on makeup, fashionable clothing, jewelry, and diet plans. And in spite of all the money and time we spend in those areas, many of us remain frustrated with the way we look. The truth is, we do not have to look like a TV commercial or magazine ad to be beautiful. We are designed by God so we must be BEAUTIFUL and the best!

We have an outrageous blessing bestowed upon us according to Genesis 1:26-27. It tells us we are made in the image and likeness of God. Unfortunately, too many women give lip service only to this powerful truth without allowing it to penetrate their total being. We spend too much time seeking our security and personal worth in world sources: personal success, status, beauty, wealth, and the approval of others. I know because I have been there. But praise God, I know the **Truth**, the Word of God, and it has set me free.

God's desire is for women to come forth into new life. The worldly rewards we spend so much time seeking will fulfill us for only a short time, often rewards lead us to a false sense of who we are, and can lead us into thinking we always need approval. When we base our security on success and others' opinions, we become dependent on our abilities to perform and please others. This can result in a stronghold, and we are working to eliminate those from our life. We must constantly apply the **Truths** that can motivate us to live for Christ rather than for the approval of other people.

Christ is the source of our security, the basis of our worth, and the only one who promises and never fails. The enemy works at deceiving us into believing that our self-worth equals performance plus others' opinions. He feeds our minds with junk because he is the father of lies as indicated in John 8:44. If he can succeed in keeping our minds on worldly things, then he succeeds in keeping our minds off Christ.

The Bible tells us to seek first the kingdom of heaven and all else will be given to us (Matthew 6:33). God is the solution! He has given us His Word so that we do not have to be enslaved by the tricks of the enemy. We are created in God's image, and that is where our self-worth is. Our real beauty cannot be bought, added on, hung from our ears, or laid on our neck. Our real strength and completeness should come from Christ. Christ lives in us and that dictates being BEAUTIFUL and the best.

Forsake the world's lies and replace them with God's viewpoint. The Word of God is the true and accurate roadmap for our life, and we must use it daily to live a Christ-like life.

Confidently say to yourself:

• I am created by God, and what He created was very good. "Then God saw everything that He had made, and indeed it was very good." Genesis 1:31

• I am created in God's image. "So God created man in His own image; in the image of God He created him; male and female He created them." Genesis 1:27

• I am a wonderful creation. "For You formed my inward parts; You covered me in my mother's womb. I will praise You, for I am fearfully and wonderfully made; marvelous are Your works and that my soul knows very well." Psalm 139:13-14

• I am the temple for God's Spirit. "Do you not know that you are the temple of God and that the Spirit of God dwells in you?" I Corinthians 3:16

• I know God values the heart more than appearance "...For the Lord does not see as man sees; for man looks at the outward appearance, but the Lord looks at the heart." I Samuel 16:7b

If we know who we are inside, no matter what we look like on the outside, we will know that we are designed by God so we must be BEAUTIFUL and the best. Remember to keep the **Truth** flowing in your mind, mood, and attitude. Pursue God's Word frequently as you continue to develop your personal relationship with the Lord. Tell yourself the truth and ask the Holy Spirit to cleanse your soul, flush out the world's opinions, and replace them with spiritual realities. We are BEAUTIFUL and the BEST.

In what ways can others see the beauty of God reflected through you?

FROM GOD'S HEART TO YOURS

Genesis 1:26,27
Psalm 139:13,14

From Your Heart to God's
R E F L E C T I O N S

Encouragement Four

Don't Be Vogue on the Outside and Vague on the Inside

Encouragement Four
Don't Be Vogue on the Outside and Vague on the Inside

*H*ave you ever entered a room and saw beautiful, well adorned women who you thought had everything going for them? You looked and saw beautiful St. John suits, Liz Claiborne dresses, Gucci shoes, LV bags, and John Hardy jewelry. You think to yourself, *they are truly vogue on the outside.* As you make your way through the crowd and begin to talk with the ladies, you are amazed at how in-style, fashionable, popular trend setters they are outwardly, but they are clearly not defined within. They are vogue on the outside and vague on the inside.

Many of us fall into that category when it comes to our spiritual lives. We can quote scripture, tell you all the latest Christian books and current TV ministries, but we gossip, complain, cheat, and go on and on. We put on masks, wear beautiful and oftentimes very expensive clothing and makeup, get our hair done weekly, and we

31

are hurting, angry, disappointed, confused, and some-times even depressed on the inside.

People, objects, success, goals, and other desires all compete for priority in our lives. Too often, any one of these things can quickly bump God right out of His first place if we do not actively choose to give Him first place in every area of our life. We can be ever so in vogue and out of touch with God—vague on the inside.

As daughters of the King of Kings, we do not have to be only vogue on the outside. We can cry out to the Lord as David did in Psalm 51:10, "Create in me a clean heart, O God, and renew a steadfast spirit within me." We have to change our convictions from worldly convictions to God-centered convictions. This means we must have the mind of Christ as referenced in Philippians 2:5. We have to align our thoughts with the mind of Christ.

Living under the guidance of the Holy Spirit will move us from being vogue on the outside and vague on the inside. By obeying the leading of the Holy Spirit, those fleshly inclinations that we all have will be defeated. It is God's spirit that we want checking our motives because our minds can play tricks on us. We have become pros at training our minds to go in the direction we desire, often allowing ourselves to approve behaviors that are not aligned to the mind of Christ.

Recognize the nudging of the Holy Spirit by checking your motives always, seeking God's presence regularly, praying consistently, and being totally committed to becoming more like Christ. I Corinthians 2:10 tells us, "… the Spirit searches all things, yes, the deep things of God." Do not rely on the things of the world to define you, for greater is the Spirit of God that lives in you than the things of the world. Flow with the leading of the Holy Spirit. I promise it works.

In what ways are you stepping in vogue with the world, yet out of step with the Holy Spirit?

From Your Heart to God's
R E F L E C T I O N S

Encouragement Five

Avoid Emotional Bankruptcy
(It's A High Price for Low Living)

Encouragement Five
Avoid Emotional Bankruptcy
(It's A High Price for Low Living)

*M*any of us have been or are currently lost in the fog of fear, obligation, and/or guilt, whether on the receiving end or giving it out. It could be fear of loss, fear of change, fear of rejection, fear of losing power, fear of not being linked to someone or something; it can be fear of anything. It is our own personal fear.

Obligation often forces us into a stance of doing what those closest to us want us to do, even if it means our unhappiness. And guilt misplaced comes over us because of the skepticism we have established in our minds. I can identify with the fear of obligation and guilt. In years past, I allowed both of them to emotionally blackmail me, and I wondered why I was emotionally bankrupted. No more, because I am free and who the Lord sets free is free indeed (John 8:36)! I want you to experience this liberation, too, on this side of heaven.

The enemy loves to keep us wrapped up, tied up, and tangled up emotionally. This robs us of our confidence in the power of God to give us victory, and it diminishes our potential to move into a more personal relationship with the Lord. Reach out to the King of Kings and Lord of Lords; learn the Truth and be set free from emotional bankruptcy.

We are very dependent upon emotional support. Have you ever said, "I am just emotionally drained" or "I cannot give another inch"? We can feel this way, yet move forward on doing what we really don't want to do because someone else expects us to do it. That is what I call emotional bankruptcy. It can happen when we are trying to get something from someone or someone is trying to get something from us. Our emotions are an easy target. Oftentimes, emotional bankruptcy is the result of emotional blackmail. It can happen with your spouse, boss, mother, sister, children, father, best friend, or others. As a matter of fact, those who are emotional blackmailers are usually people whom we love and cherish.

What happens is that we live in fear of not doing what someone wants us to do or not being what someone wants us to be. We forget that fear is the opposite of faith. How does it work? I'm glad you asked. Have you ever heard anyone say or maybe you have even said, "If you loved me, you would do such and such"; "After all, I have always been there for you"; "I have done all this for you, and you cannot even..."; "That is okay, I will get someone who really cares to help me out?" You get the picture. This is called manipulation, and we all have used it or had someone use it on us.

Not all manipulation is troublesome; it becomes emotional blackmail when it is used repeatedly to coerce someone into complying with the blackmailer's demands. Sometimes we blackmail ourselves because of the things we tell ourselves or hear others say, and we take it as being true. As a man thinks in his heart, so is he (Proverbs 23:7). Once we yank out the irrationalities and untruths from our thoughts and replace them with the Truth, we can live rich and fulfilling emotional lives. The Word of God holds all Truths.

When we recognize we are emotionally bankrupted and the reason why (because we are being emotionally blackmailed), then we can become new creatures and old things will pass away (II Corinthians 5:17). Measure your success by the measure of the character of Christ you possess. Do not allow the sun to go down with you being angry. Be an exhorter by building others up. Be kind and compassionate to others. Forgive others just as Christ has forgiven you. Recognize and accept the promises of God.

Take off the blinders today and receive your sight, for the truth is what sets us free. This is a moment for healing. Call out to Jesus right now as the blind man did in Luke 18:38-42, and by faith be restored. The Son of Righteousness is waiting; behold His image, grab His hand, and walk in His likeness. Being an emotional blackmailer or a victim of emotional blackmail is not in His likeness, and we want to walk in His likeness.

What fear-based blinders must you remove to enrich your spiritual wealth?

FROM GOD'S HEART TO YOURS

John 8:36

From Your Heart to God's
R E F L E C T I O N S

Encouragement Six
Open Your Eyes: Refocus, Regroup, and Press On

Encouragement Six

Open Your Eyes: Refocus, Regroup, and Press On

*I*n the mist of our pathologically fast-paced society, God calls us to get a grip on our lives. We are called to move from imbalance to a place where God has control of every aspect of our lives. Trying to balance work, family, and a career in our insanely busy world may seem close to impossible. It seems the pressure to move faster, produce more, and accomplish greater things never lets up, and with that, things can get out of balance.

Stop right now and be honest with yourself; admit that there are some areas of your life that are out of balance. The balancing act involves different choices and difficult choices. Many are staggering under the load of "shoulds" life piles on us: career, home, relationships, children, activities, ministry, exercise, and on and on. Some devote too much time to vocational pursuits; others invest excessive time to recreational pursuits; many are giving too much attention to people and things that are draining; still others are consumed with personal advancements and have little time for family, friends, and spiritual needs.

Behind much of our life's imbalance lurk a couple of questions: Is God trustworthy? Can God be trusted to provide what we most deeply need, or do we have to wear ourselves out making our own provisions? The Word of God tells us to seek first the kingdom of heaven and His righteousness, and all things will be added to us (Matthew 6:33); for when we delight ourselves in the Lord, He will give us the desires of our heart (Psalm 37:4).

When the bottom is falling out and things are out of balance, what should you do? Blame someone else? No, that makes you bitter. Wallow in self-pity? No, that only paralyzes you and alienates those around you. Rely on "what if" or "if only"? No, that only makes you depressed. Life will throw curves, and when that happens, we must open our spiritual ears and eyes: refocus, regroup, and press on! It is all about how we deal with it that makes the difference; it is all about our response to the situation. Come to the Lord when burdened and He will give you rest (Matthew 11:28).

Our priorities determine how we spend our time, so we must be prayerful in setting them. There are many things contending for our time and attention. Start your day with asking God to help you prioritize your to do list. Begin by saying, "Today, I will prioritize my life according to God's will, and I will give my energies to those things that help me fulfill it." That might mean getting up a little earlier in the morning and spending time with the Lord before beginning your day. I have found this to set the most positive tone for my days.

There is a war going on in this world, and it is very much like the war in which we find ourselves on any given day when we experience overload. Our life gets out of balance and we feel weak. Yes, it is a spiritual war, and we have to be prepared for it; refocus, regroup, and press on by putting on the whole armor (Ephesians 6:13-18).

- Gird your waist with the truth.
- Put on the breastplate of righteousness.
- Shod your feet with the preparation of the gospel of peace.
- Take up the shield of faith.
- Put on the helmet of salvation.
- Take up the sword of the Spirit—the Word of God.
- Pray always.

Follow through, and you will find yourself experiencing supernatural strength and victory in Jesus. Fight in the strength of the Lord, which comes from the Holy Spirit. Pray that God will sharpen your spiritual ears and eyes, touch your heart, and guide you to refocus, regroup, and press on.

Which aspect of the spiritual armor do you most need to attend to right now?

FROM GOD'S HEART TO YOURS

Ephesians 6:13-18

From Your Heart to God's
R E F L E C T I O N S

Encouragement Seven

Be of Good Cheer: Seasons Come and Seasons Go

Encouragement Seven
Be of Good Cheer: Seasons Come and Seasons Go

*T*hink of the seasons of life in relationship to the four seasons that we experience from winter to fall. In the winter of life, we are refined; in the spring of life, we are renewed; in the summer of life, we rest; and in the fall of life, we reflect. How are you doing in each of your seasons? Our God is a seasonal God; everything has its time as reflected in Ecclesiastes 3:1.

Think about your journey in life thus far and see the seasons you have experienced:

  • Winter is cold, lifeless, and dead. It is a time for refining. The flowers are not blooming, the frost sets in, and the skies become cloudy.
  • Spring warms up a bit, brings hope, and budding emerges. It is a time for renewal—it marks a season for planting and growing; flowers bloom and birds sing.
  • Summer is even warmer; it is fruitful, blessings come, and things grow greener. It is a time of rest—it follows spring and marks an increase in

growth; it is a time for nurturing and easy living.
• Fall leads to fading, weakening, and cooling in
the atmosphere. It is a time of reflection—it
brings chillness in the air, activities slow down,
and the focus changes; with fall comes a new
perspective.

What season are you in? We all go through them, just
taking the time and realizing your season can mean
victory in your thinking.

In John 16:33, Jesus warned us that we would have
winter seasons in our lives when He said, "In the world
ye shall have tribulation, but be of good cheer, I have
overcome the world." The season cycle is inevitable and
very necessary because each season matures us in the
things of God. Be persistent, learn to recognize the
signs and always look for the positive in every season of
your life.

God is faithful, and in due season, our blessings will
come if we humble ourselves under the mighty hand of
the Father (I Peter 5:6-7). Remember, seasons are time
frames that are allotted for something to happen. In
order to take advantage of the benefits that a season has
for us, we should ask God to show us the right things to
do during that season. When He reveals to us what to
do, then we have to be obedient and do it.

Seasons come and seasons go so be sure to tune to
God's weather channel daily:
• Winter skies—Psalm 121:1-2: I will lift up mine
eyes unto the hills—from whence cometh my
help? My help comes from the Lord, who made
heaven and earth.
• Winter windchill factor—Psalm 30:5: Weeping

may endure for a night, but joy comes in the morning.

• Spring forecast—Psalm 118:24: This is the day the Lord has made; we will rejoice and be glad in it.

• Spring showers of blessing—Malachi 3:10-11: If I will not open for you the windows of heaven, and pour out for you such blessing that there will not be room enough to receive it. And I will rebuke the devourer for your sakes.

• Summer sunrise—Malachi 1:11: ...from the rising of the sun, even to its going down, My name shall be great...

• Summer heat wave—II Corinthians 4:8: We are hard-pressed on every side, yet not crushed; we are perplexed, but not in despair; persecuted, but not forsaken; struck down, but not destroyed.

• Fall outlook—II Chronicles 16:9a: For the eyes of the Lord run to and fro throughout the whole earth, to show Himself strong on behalf of those whose heart is loyal to Him.

• Fall atmosphere pressure point—Isaiah 59:19: ...when the enemy comes in like a flood, the Spirit of the Lord will lift up a standard against him.

Seasons come and seasons go; watch for the signs in your life and know what to do. Reflect on the promises of God and tune in to God's weather channel daily. Expand your personal relationship with the Lord and get to know Him better by getting into the Word of God as you continue to mature spiritually through the seasons of life.

What season of life are you in? What are you preparing to harvest?

From Your Heart to God's
R E F L E C T I O N S

Encouragement Eight
Plant What You Want to Harvest

Encouragement Eight
Plant What You Want to Harvest

ou would not plant okra and expect to reap tomatoes. When we plant carrots, we expect to get carrots. It is a natural law to reap what we sow. The harvest is always the product of the seed. The basic rules that apply in the soil of the garden, also apply in the soil of our soul. You and I plant seeds every day, and what we plant is what we'll harvest. We harvest on this side of heaven, in the here-and-now, and eternally, in the then-and-there.

Christians have two gardens in which we can sow, that of the flesh and that of the Spirit. The person who sows in her own flesh dwells in her own desires instead of letting the Spirit subdue the flesh. Sin is centered in the flesh, and we are in a constant war between the flesh and the Spirit. If we sow to the flesh, we reap destruction. If we sow to the Spirit, we reap blessings. Paul says do not be deceived, God is not mocked; for whatever a man sows, that he will also reap (Galatians 6:7).

Every one of us has options. If we sow good seeds, we get a good harvest. If we sow bad seeds, we get a corrupted harvest. Whatever is sown, whether it is physical, natural, or spiritual, can only reproduce itself. At this stage in my life, I want to reap the good, so I have chosen to sow more good. What about you? What is your harvest looking like? What have you been sowing lately? Sowing to the flesh robs us of joy, but sowing to the Spirit reaps blessings. We cannot expect to sow betrayal and reap trust, sow discord and reap unity, sow sin and reap sanctification, sow hypocrisy and reap holiness in life.

If we sow to the flesh, we reap corruption:

- Abraham sowed to the flesh and harvested Ishmael.
- Isaac sowed to the flesh and reaped Esau.
- David sowed to the flesh and reaped a rebellious son.
- Solomon sowed to the flesh and reaped blindness and bondage.

On the other hand, if we sow to the Spirit, we reap a blessing:

- Abraham sowed to the Spirit and harvested Isaac.
- Hannah sowed to the Spirit and reaped Samuel.
- David sowed to the Spirit and reaped a royal covenant.
- Peter sowed to the Spirit and reaped Pentecost.

To sow to the Spirit is the same as walking by the Spirit so we produce the Fruit of the Spirit as outlined in Galatians 5:16-25. It is the same as abiding in Christ and having His Word abide in us (John 8:31, 15:7). It is the same as giving our body as a living and holy sacrifice, acceptable to God, and not being conformed to this world, but being transformed by the renewing of our minds, that we may prove what the will of God is that which is good and acceptable, and perfect (Romans 12:1-2).

Did you know that the way to get what we want from others is to give to others what they need? Think about that in relationship to yourself. How does it fit into the principle of sowing and reaping? Easily!

- If you want more friends, be a friend.
- If you want more understanding from others, be more understanding to others.
- If you want to be rich, give.
- If you want to be poor, grasp.
- If you want abundance, scatter.
- If you want to be needy, hoard.

The law operates both negatively and positively; the more one sows to the flesh, the more she will reap the corruption which the flesh alone can produce (Galatians 6:8). He who sows sparingly will also reap sparingly, and he who sows bountifully, will also reap bountifully (II Corinthians 9:6).

There is a time for sowing and a time for reaping. We will enjoy the fruits of our labor in God's time. We might grow tired, weary, and disappointed, but we must keep on sowing good—knowing that God will bring our harvest to pass. We cannot harvest until the seed is sown, we cannot harvest until the seed is cultivated, and we cannot get a harvest until the seed is ripe. But, we will always get a harvest in the season it is due (Galatians 6:9). Keep the right attitude and speak the right words and the law of the harvest will produce in due season.

Ask God to provide His perfect will for you, in His perfect time, and be careful what you sow.

What seeds are you planting in your garden as you interact with family, friends, and colleagues?

From Your Heart to God's
R E F L E C T I O N S

Encouragement Nine

Redefine Success: Walk In God's Will and God's Way

Encouragement Nine

Redefine Success: Walk In God's Will and God's Way

*G*od wants us to be successful and has built into each of us the desire to be successful. Jeremiah 29:11 tells us the Lord's thoughts toward us are of peace and a future of hope. The nature of God is to provide for His children abundantly. Just look at I Corinthians 2:9, "Eyes have not seen, nor ears heard, nor have entered into the heart of man the things God has prepared for those who love Him." He has put His principles for success in the Bible so that we can learn and use them. The problem is, we too often seek success as defined by the world rather than by God.

The world tends to sum up success in terms of fame and fortune, but God sums it up in terms of relationships, character, and obedience. His desire is for us to succeed first and foremost in our personal relationship with Him, and next in our relationship with others. God delights in leading us when we seek Him with our heart (Jeremiah 29:13). So that means we must be intimate with God in order to build our relationship with Him.

71

We have to be God-focused and not self-focused. Take a minute and reflect and see where you fall:

- SELF-FOCUSED—Self-made, self-defined, and self-gratified
- GOD-FOCUSED—Begins with God's plan and purpose, God, God, God
- SELF-FOCUSED—Involved primarily with success that is measured in terms of awards, dollars, clothing, status, and position
- GOD-FOCUSED—Involved primarily with success that is defined in terms of eternal purpose, spiritual benefits, Godly character, and obedience to God's expectations

If we put our faith in ourselves and our abilities, intellect and vision, our foundation is only as strong as we are. Putting our faith in God is what makes our foundation strong. Our goal is to build our success on solid foundation. Do not fall into the world's trap of becoming a self-focused individual. We want to do God's will and God's way, get intimate with Him, and follow His roadmap—the Bible.

We know that we are to love our neighbors, our enemies, and bless those who might even be against us, as outlined in Matthew 5:44. We have to take a look at our attitudes and behavior toward other people and treat them as God would have us do. If you are not sure what those requirements are, search the Word of God for answers and pray for the leading of the Holy Spirit.

If we want to experience and enjoy success as God defines it, we must learn to be obedient to His will and His way. It means hearing and moving when God speaks to us. That is why we have to know Him for ourselves. Think about Ruth who chose to go with her mother-in-law to a foreign land. She trusted God with her whole heart to be her refuge, and she did not rely on herself (Ruth 2:12). She followed the leading of her mother-in-law, who was a Godly women, and Ruth found favor (Ruth 2:13-16). Blessings of obedience are immeasurable. Isaiah 1:19 tells us if we are willing and obedient, we shall eat the good of the land.

Faith that obeys is God's key that unlocks countless blessings. If we want to enjoy success as God defines it, we must learn to be obedient to His will and His way. This means releasing our own plans, pride, and will and seeking God's plan and purpose for our success. Get intimate with the Father, build Godly relationships, and be obedient to the leading of the Holy Spirit; that is God's will and God's way for experiencing success.

If you do not know Jesus as your personal Savior, get to know Him right now, and accept Christ as your Savior and Lord: Admit your sins and repent, believe Christ is the Son of God and that He died for your sins (John 3:16), and commit your life to God.

What steps can you take to redefine success for yourself—God's way?

FROM GOD'S HEART TO YOURS

Jeremiah 29:11-13

From Your Heart to God's
R E F L E C T I O N S

Encouragement Ten
Explore Promise, Purpose, and Pain

Encouragement Ten

Explore Promise, Purpose, and Pain

We all have a purpose on this earth. As we walk in our purpose, life takes us through very interesting and dynamic experiences—experiences that we should learn to accept and grow from. It starts with a promise, then a purpose, and sometimes even pain. The beauty of it all is that no matter what, God's promises will always prevail. We just have to stay connected to Him.

My eyes have been opened to many truths and revelations over the past years as I have sought the Lord for His perfect will for my life. My relationship with the Lord has grown because I spend time with Him in prayer, praise, worship, and meditation. It is my desire to become closer and closer to Christ, to become more like Him in character and action, and to explore His promises and purpose for my life.

There are three specific lessons I have learned during my journey down the avenue of promise, purpose, and pain. It is my prayer that your spiritual eyes and ears will be opened to the revelation knowledge God has for you as I share these lessons.

Lesson 1 - Running ahead of God is never a good idea.
We have a tendency too often to run ahead of God when we feel that things are not moving fast enough or when we simply want to control circumstances or people. Because God has given us free will, God does not always stop our actions; neither does He always save us from the consequences of those actions.

Perhaps it is pride that makes us feel we must take control of situations; in fact, many Bible scholars say that pride is the root of all other sins. Of course, it is appropriate for us to take the initiative in many situations, but never without praying for direction and being willing to wait for the answer. Wait on the Lord and be of good courage and He shall strengthen our heart (Psalm 27:14). Take it from me; I have learned to release control over people and things, and I am still a work in progress.

Lesson 2 - Lack of faith and impatience are costly.
When we take our eyes off God and try to do things on our own, we often pay a high price. Impatience many times coexists with lack of faith. Again, I know because I have been there, done that. I heard Adrian Rogers once say, "Don't let your testimony be weakened because of your lack of faith or patience." God will test us to reveal weaknesses so we can grow from glory to glory to glory—for His glory. A faith that cannot be tested will not last.

Lack of faith and patience can bring hardship and pain. The Word of God is sure and final, and we can find security in living our lives by what the Word says regardless of the way circumstances appear. I always encourage myself and others to keep our eyes on the Mountain Mover and not the mountain. I try practicing this daily, and I know that it is a life-long journey for all of us. I have learned that no matter what difficulties and delays we experience, our greatest stabilizer is our dependence upon the Lord and His Word. It takes faith to receive the promises God has ordained for us, and it takes patience and character to maintain what He has given us.

Be assured that we will face continued difficulties. Proverbs 3:5 promises us that if we trust in the Lord with all our heart, and lean not to our own understanding; in all our ways acknowledge Him, and He will direct your paths. Commit your ways to the Lord, trust also in Him, and He shall direct our path. As we know, man makes his plans and God orders his steps (Proverbs 16:9).

Lesson 3 - Submission yields a prize.

The life we live is much bigger than us. It is never about us! God has orchestrated things in such a way that our daily dependence has to be on Him alone in order to yield the Fruit of the Spirit. As we draw nearer to Him, He draws nearer to us (James 4:8). We should find ourselves at some point submitting to His will, but sometimes it is after we have taken a number of detours.

Liberation is found in submission, based on my personal experiences, and I thank God that He has provided me with that revelation. I pray you have, or will find, liberation in submitting to God. Submission is our aid, not our enemy, and when we see the effect of submission on our lives, it is no wonder why God prizes it so highly.

We must continuously remind ourselves of God's promises. Take them personally, have faith in God, be patient, submit to God's will, and see things through to the end. Remember, first the promise, then the purpose, and sometimes there is the pain, but always return to the promise.

81

Ask God to make things clear to you, to give you wisdom, direction, and continued discernment in all areas of your life. Ask Him for the supernatural will to walk in submission to Him. I promise you that God will speak directly to your spirit and you will know without a shadow of a doubt that it is our Father speaking. I know because God has brought me to that point and He will do it for you because He tells us in Romans 2:11 that there is no partiality with God. What He has done for me, He will do for you. The key to receiving the promises of God is obedience. Have faith, be patient, and submit to God's will.

What is your current pain teaching you about the purpose that lies ahead?

FROM GOD'S HEART TO YOURS

Proverbs 3:5

From Your Heart to God's
R E F L E C T I O N S

Encouragement Eleven
Beware of the Pride Sting

Encouragement Eleven
Beware of the Pride Sting

*H*ave you ever wanted to get something but it was really out of your reach? I have. You know how we do; we place such a high value on our self-sufficiency. There was a woman who once saw a gray ball hanging above her porch night light, instead of getting someone to assist her, she reached for it and was suddenly swarmed by hornets. It was a hornets' nest. Beware of the pride sting.

Many times in our efforts to get things done, pride rears its ugly head and the self-sufficient, the only-I-can, syndrome kicks in and the result is a sting. I never considered myself as a prideful person until one day a sister in Christ pointed out to me that I was prideful and that it was blocking my blessings. At first I was very hurt, and then the Lord pricked my spirit and directed me to research and learn more about the concept of pride. I must admit, to my surprise, I had been stung by pride. What I learned, I hope will help you as much as it has helped me to make some changes in this area. Living for Christ is a continuous journey, but I am a better person as the result of my sister in Christ pointing out this area in my life that needed improvement.

Pride can be couched in stinging statements such as: never mind; I'll do it myself; I've got this under control; it will get done regardless; this is the best and only way; I'll just get someone else to do it; I can do it better; or we have done it this way for as long as I can remember, and we aren't going to change now. Sound familiar? Think about it for a moment. Have you ever spoken any of these statements or any that are closely related? Do you think these kinds of attitudes affect how we live out our lives? Sure they do. They have stung the life out of someone, maybe even you.

Pride takes on different forms, and sometimes we are not even conscious of it. Pride can manifest itself in either speech or demeanor. Here is how pride might look in your life; check yourself out and be honest:

Pride Can Hinder Communication
- You jump to conclusions without details.
- You pass rumors about others, trying to make them look bad so you will look good.
- You don't listen to others because you are trying to make your point.
- You must have it the way you say.

Pride Can Provoke Criticism
- You correct, judge, and evaluate others constantly.
- You criticize and tear others down.
- You find fault in others when things don't go your way.

Pride Can Prohibit Confession
- You have difficulty admitting when you are wrong.

• You have difficulty saying you are sorry and meaning it.
• You struggle with forgiving others who have wronged you.

A sting of any kind results in some form of swelling: snakes, bees, wasps, and mosquitoes all sting and the sting leaves a bump. The more we scratch or rub the bump, the more it swells, and many times it ends up being infected. That is very similar to how our egos swell, resulting in puffed up, haughty attitudes that are projected through our behaviors. And our behaviors are articulated in words and actions based on our thoughts.

We are to strive for excellence; our God is an excellent God as indicated in Job 37:23b. But, excellence must be kept in the context of holiness, in line with what God instructs. Every situation we encounter is an opportunity to choose to rely totally on God rather than our own inclinations. Too often we are relying on our own inclinations rather than God.

Pride can form the very basis of sin; all types of disobedience and rebellion types find root in pride. This means that every day we must consciously commit all of our ways and plans to the Lord. Pride has reared its ugly head throughout history, and people have felt the sting. Sometimes we are the receiver and sometimes we are the deliverer.

Pride is an excessively high opinion of oneself. It is an inward thought that outwardly parades its abilities, accomplishments, and acquaintances. In the book of Proverbs, we learn the following lessons:
• Pride goes before destruction and a haughty spirit before a fall (Proverbs 16:18).

• By pride comes nothing but strife, but with well-advised is wisdom (Proverbs 13:10).
• ...Pride and arrogance and the evil way and the perverse mouth I hate (Proverbs 8:13).
• A man's pride will bring him low, but the humble in spirit will retain honor (Proverbs 29:23).

The opposite of pride is humility. The world views humility as a sign of weakness, and the Word of God tells us over and over we are not to measure ourselves against the world standards (Romans 12:2). Seeking to be at the top is what measures your worth in the world, but the Word of God tells us the last will be first in Matthew 20:16.

Check this out and measure your success:

• Pride speaks of its own accomplishments, but humility speaks of the accomplishments of others.
• Pride puffs up itself, but humility puffs up others.
• Pride is selfish and seeks to please self, but humility seeks to provide for others.
• Pride seeks honor, but humility gives honor to others.

Jesus came into this world as a humble servant to model the way for us. Seek to mirror the character of Christ, not the way of the world.

What can you do to eliminate the pride
in your life?

FROM GOD'S HEART TO YOURS

Proverbs 21:2

From Your Heart to God's
R E F L E C T I O N S

Encouragement Twelve
Be a Servant: Christ is The Master

Encouragement Twelve
Be a Servant: Christ is The Master

I remember as a little girl people would ask me what I wanted to be when I grew up and I wanted to be wonderful at whatever job I would one day do; I wanted to be great. For a moment, I would like for you to think what Jesus would like for you to be when you grow up. I think Jesus would want us to be more like Him; be a servant.

Have you ever been in a position when you thought to yourself, why am I doing this? Have you ever responded to someone else with, "This is not my job"? I remember a time when I was asked to take the phones for several offices in my department. I thought to myself, *why don't they ask a secretary to do this; this is not my job; I do not get paid to answer the phones.* Then my heart was pricked, and I was convicted. Why not me? You see, servants go above and beyond the call of duty, for greatness is dignified in being a servant.

I cannot remember ever hearing anyone say when they grew up they wanted to be a servant. We live in an age of superstars, where everyone wants to be like someone else, someone who is rich and famous. Take Oprah Winfrey, Denzel Washington, Jamie Lee Curtis, Ted Kennedy, Barack Obama, or Tom Cruise for example.

They pose in the spotlight, and we credit them as being great entertainers, actors, talk show hosts, politicians, etc. And I would agree that many of them are, but the question is, what is the standard by which we measure greatness? The world measures greatness by what you have and who you are rubbing shoulders with. The greatness in women like Oprah Winfrey comes not from her riches, but from her willingness to use those blessings to serve others. By God's standards, the greatness of all are those who serve (Matthew 20:28). Do you want to be great? Serve others.

Jesus tells us that those who desire to be great, let them serve; just like Him who came not to be served but to serve (Matthew 20:26-28). Consider Jesus' fellowship in John 13:4-5 when he washed the feet of the disciples. He set an example for us of what it means to be great. Jesus measured greatness in terms of service, not status. Serving means being available when there is a need, and there is always a need. How available are you? And when available, what are your motives—is it for public service or public glory? It should always be for the glory of God.

We should look for ways to support, build up, encourage, and stimulate others. Be a giver instead of a getter; be a forgiver instead of a grudge holder; be a forgetter instead of a score keeper; be great and serve.

How do you reflect the attitude and characteristic of Christ in your good works?

FROM GOD'S HEART TO YOURS

Matthew 20:26-28

From Your Heart to God's
R E F L E C T I O N S

Encouragement Thirteen

Practice Gentleness

Encouragement Thirteen

Practice Gentleness

*W*hen is the last time you examined your fruit of gentleness? It is something we sometimes just take for granted, but we should not. The fact is, gentleness is more needed today than perhaps ever before because we live in such a violent world.

What does it mean to be gentle? The Greek language, in which the New Testament was originally written, was a precise and expressive language. When the Greeks developed a word, they not only gave it a careful definition, but they almost always illustrated it.

Their definition of gentleness was "power under control," and they illustrated it with the picture of a horse that had been tamed. Gentleness to them was a powerful animal with its power completely under control. So when you think about gentleness, think about "power under control"—anger under control, jealousy and envy under control, gossip under control, our emotions ALL under God's control.

Jesus is our perfect example. Let's consider three events in His life that demonstrate the gentleness of Jesus, that same gentleness He wants to see displayed in us.

In the fourth chapter of the Gospel of John, we see His gentleness in the familiar story about the woman at the well. Keeping in mind the culture of the day—a man did not talk publicly to a woman and a Jewish person certainly did not associate with Samaritans. So if Jesus had been the normal Jewish man, He would never have spoken to her. But Jesus was deliberately trying to break down the barriers between the two groups. We are often faced with barriers, and as Christians, we are to work at breaking them down.

The Samaritan woman at the well taunts Jesus and speaks rather unkindly to Him. Yet Jesus responds gently to her. He sees a thirsty, needy person and He offers her living water that will quench her thirst, not for a moment, but forever. What a gentle approach!

There is a similar story found in John 8, a story of the woman who was caught in the act of adultery. Yes, guilty as charged, and Jesus could have judged her harshly. But, Jesus treats her gently. He writes in the sand and shames her accusers into slinking away. Then He says to her, "Neither do I condemn thee. Go your way and sin no more." What a gentle approach!

Still another story in Luke 19, where Zacchaeus, the wee little man who gets all his self-esteem from taking money from other people, talks with Jesus. He is rich and dishonest, but Jesus looks at him and tells Zacchaeus to come down, that He is coming to his house. Soon we see a changed Zacchaeus and we hear Jesus telling him that this day salvation has come to this house.

Let me suggest that we aim at being as gentle as Jesus. He is about building relationships just as His Father, for God is relational to His core. Women, too, are relational. We care more about relationships than just about anything else. Let us work at restoring those who are broken.

The model for sharing our faith is gentleness. Gentleness is what helps us reach those who do not know the Lord. Gentleness is what helps us have unity among ourselves (the church). When we allow the Holy Spirit to produce the fruit of gentleness in our lives, we will be able to make more of a difference than ever before in sharing our faith, in cooperating with our friends, in being honest with one another, in receiving righteous criticism, and in living successfully.

The Holy Spirit gives us the fruit of gentleness (strength under control) to create a graciousness in us that combats any tendency to be harsh with people. Paul tells us to live with complete lowliness of mind (humility) and meekness (unselfishness, gentleness, mildness), with patience, bearing with one another and making allowances because we love one another. Ask the Lord to give you more of a Christ-like graciousness that springs from a gentle and humble heart in all your relationships. Continue to be more like Christ in all your ways.

How do you relate to gentleness? How do you pursue it, put it on, practice it, and give it to others?

FROM GOD'S HEART TO YOURS

Galatians 5:22-25

Encouragement Fourteen

Soar Like an Eagle

Encouragement Fourteen

Soar Like an Eagle

*D*o you want to fly high in the Lord? Then wait on the Lord, for those who wait shall renew their strength, mount up with wings as eagles, and will run and not be weary (Isaiah 40:31). We wait for traffic lights to turn green, we wait for trains to pass by, we wait in the bank line, we wait for our turn in the beauty salon, and wait for food to cook. Certainly, if we can wait on those things, we can wait on the Lord.

If we want to experience the glory of God more, we must wait on the Lord. God wants to lift us all to higher places in Him, but we must learn to wait on Him. We might get weary in waiting, but the Lord has promised to renew our strength if we wait for Him. We have to develop eagle strength and character so that we can fly high in the Lord.

Think about the eagle. It is a remarkable, majestic bird that has tremendous character and strength, beginning with its wings. An eagle soars to higher heights just by its wings' spread. It is effortless for the eagle because God has given the eagle a special talent, just as He has given each of us.

In the Bible, the eagle is used as a simile and a simile connects two unlike things by drawing comparisons using the word like or as. For example, you might tell your son, "You're just like your daddy" or you might say, "She struts like a peacock" or "She's as lovely as a rose." You get the idea.

The Bible tells us that those who wait on the Lord will renew their strength and mount as eagles. I love being compared to an eagle and to work at acquiring their characteristics and strength. Eagles fly at an outstanding altitude; they soar high, survive weather conditions, and have a keen ability to watch and observe.

One thing that astounds me the most about eagles is how they can survive without food for long periods. It is like fasting is for us, and we know fasting is the most powerful spiritual discipline of all Christian disciplines. Surviving without food for several days is common with eagles, particularly when they go through molting, which is a process they go through to replace their feathers each year. It is their most depressed period because they lose virtually everything; they are almost incapacitated. Most birds that go through this process do not make it, but the eagle lies there and rests until it is renewed.

Turbulent winds give the eagle great lifting power, which causes the eagle to fly higher, have a larger view of low lands, use less effort to get to the top, and allows the eagle to fly faster and stay higher longer.

When we liken it to the life of a believer, like it or not; there will be periods of molting. The good news is that we can possess supernatural strength to survive these times by waiting on the Lord. The eagle only reaches its full potential by how it handles the adversities that come. How do we make it through our adversities? We wait on the Lord as we actively pursue His presence— His intimacy and interaction.

How do we accomplish waiting on the Lord? We mount up on eagle's wings and:
- Meditate on the Word.
- Make no provision for the flesh.
- Recognize and be obedient to the prompting of the Holy Spirit.
- Know that this, too, shall pass.

When trials and tribulations come, be like an eagle and rise above the situation and circumstance, for discipline in adversity brings us into our full potential. Trust in the Lord with all your heart and lean not to your own understanding; in all your ways acknowledge Him and He will direct your path (Proverbs 3:5-6).

We can learn a lot from the eagle; adopt the character and strength of the eagle and fly high in the Lord. Mount up on wings as an eagle, spread your wings, and soar to higher heights in Jesus, from glory to glory. The Lord will renew, refresh, and replace our strength.

How can you run and not get weary?

FROM GOD'S HEART TO YOURS

Isaiah 40:31

111

From Your Heart to God's
R E F L E C T I O N S

Encouragement Fifteen

Answer the Call

Encouragement Fifteen
Answer the Call

*I*n making a difference, each of our roles can look different. Your role or ministry is unique because God wants something special from you. God has wired each of us for service, a distinctive service based on our talent(s) and gift(s). Everyone cannot be in the forefront, but everyone has a front to minister from. Remember that God wants us to be open to His directions. He often does not call the qualified; He qualifies those that He calls for such a time as this.

Some would protest that they never had a dramatic encounter or call like Mary, Paul, Jonah, Moses, or Isaiah. They all had extraordinary lives as a result of their relationship with God. All relationships with God are different, but nonetheless important in God's view. Each one of us can make a difference in this world for the glory of God.

Before you toss this thought aside and say to yourself, "Nah, that is for someone else because I cannot make a difference." Stop and reflect on the classic lines penned by Edward Everett Hale over a century ago:

I am only one.
But still I am one.
I cannot do everything.
But still I can do something.
And because I cannot do everything,
I will not refuse to do something that I can do.

A call is a pressing question—an urge that will not go away until you satisfy it. You are called for such a time as this! Step up, reach out, and bring in those who want to know what you know. Tell them that this little light of yours will shine, and let it shine, let it shine. God loves you and so do I.

What is the call that you now must answer?

FROM GOD'S HEART TO YOURS

Esther 4:14

From Your Heart to God's
R E F L E C T I O N S

A Word of Thanks

*I*t is an honor and privilege to have shared with you the thoughts that God gave me to give to you. I desire to do the will of God and His law is within my heart! My life has been transformed since I started to know God more personally. I thank God for allowing me the opportunity to connect with you—heart to heart.

As the illustration on the front cover indicates, we are all connected in spirit and Truth—heart to heart. Jesus died for our sins as indicated by the cross within the larger heart and the larger heart represents the heart of God. God spoke words of encouragement to me, and I am represented by one of the smaller hearts; I shared the encouragements with you, and you are represented by the other smaller heart. Finally, God speaks to you, and then you speak to God as you journal your thoughts.

There is nothing higher than Truth and the Truth triumphs over everything and everyone. All scriptures are based on Truth. Thank you for taking the time to see, hear, and know God better; He is The Truth.

Always in His Love,

Donnella

FROM GOD'S HEART TO YOURS

Psalm 40:8

*Let the words of my mouth and the
meditation of my heart be acceptable in
Your sight, O Lord, my strength and
my Redeemer.*

Psalm 19:14

FROM GOD'S HEART TO YOURS

Scriptures on Encouragement

For God so loved the world that He gave His only begotten Son, that whoever believes in Him should not perish but have everlasting life.
John 3:16

God is faithful, by whom you were called into the fellowship of His Son, Jesus Christ our Lord.
I Corinthians 1:9

God is light and in Him is no darkness at all.
I John 1:5b

The Lord is good to those who wait for Him, to the soul who seeks Him.
Lamentations 3:25

Many are the afflictions of the righteous, but the Lord delivers him out of them all.
Psalm 34:19

Therefore humble yourselves under the mighty hand of God, that He may exalt you in due time, casting all your care upon Him, for He cares for you.
I Peter 5:6-7

A man's heart plans his way, but the Lord directs his steps.
Proverbs 16:9

The preparations of the heart belong to man, but the answer of the tongue is from the Lord.
Proverbs 16:1

Wait on the Lord; be of good courage, and He shall strengthen your heart. Wait, I say on the Lord!
    Psalm 27:14

So God created man in His own image; in the image of God He created him; male and female He created them.
    Genesis 1:27

Delight yourself also in the Lord, and He shall give you the desires of your heart.
    Psalm 37:4

For it is God who works in you both to will and to do for His good pleasure.
    Philippians 2:13

Stand fast therefore in the liberty by which Christ has made us free, and do not be entangled again with a yoke of bondage.
    Galatians 5:1

Trust in the Lord with all your heart and lean not on your own understanding; in all your ways acknowledge Him and He shall direct your paths.
    Proverbs 3:5-6

For the Lord does not see as man sees; for man looks at the outward appearance, but the Lord looks at the heart.
    I Samuel 16:7b

For I know the thoughts that I think toward you, says the Lord, thoughts of peace and not of evil, to give you a future and a hope.
    Jeremiah 29:11

Every way of a man is right in his own eyes, but the Lord weighs the hearts.
   Proverbs 21:2

Finally, brethren, whatever things are true, whatever things are noble, whatever things are just, whatever things are pure, whatever things are lovely, whatever things are of good report, if there is any virtue and if there is anything praiseworthy—mediate on these things.
   Philippians 4:8

For as many of you as were baptized into Christ have put on Christ.
   Galatians 3:27

I praise You, for I am fearfully and wonderfully made; marvelous are Your works, and that my soul knows very well.
   Psalm 139:14

Therefore if the Son makes you free, you shall be free indeed.
   John 8:36

But those who wait on the Lord shall renew their strength; they shall mount up with wings like eagles, they shall run and not be weary, they shall walk and not faint.
   Isaiah 40:31

Fear not, for I am with you; be not dismayed, for I am your God. I will strengthen you, yes, I will help you. I will uphold you with My righteous right hand.
   Isaiah 41:10

To everything there is a season, a time for every purpose under heaven.
Ecclesiastes 3:1

The steps of a good man are ordered by the Lord, and He delights in his way.
Psalm 37:23

And let us not grow weary while doing good, for in due season we shall reap if we do not lose heart.
Galatians 6:9

I delight to do Your will, O my God, and your law is within my heart.
Psalm 40:8

FROM GOD'S HEART TO YOURS

About the Author

*O*ver the years, Donnella Cranford has fulfilled a desire to serve and edify others by her involvement in church, other organizations, and an established career as an educator. Her hunger to reach women beyond her local community came to fruition when she established Women After God's Own Heart (WAGOH) Ministry, Inc. in 1998.

Minister Cranford's mission is to empower, encourage, and edify women of all ages. Her foundational philosophy is that marriages, families, and communities can withstand the challenges of our world today through women who are anchored in the Word of God.

Through WAGOH Ministry, Cranford provides outreach services and mentoring to women of all ages, walks of life, church affiliations, and denominations. With a focus on illuminating the spiritual beauty of all women through basic Christian principles and values, Cranford's ministry aspires to close the gap between races, generations, cultures, and denominations.

Inspired by the biblical book of Esther, Minister Cranford established Debutantes 4 Christ as a mentoring program for teenage girls. By participating in a year-long program, young ladies begin to change their lives as they learn to mirror the character of Christ.

Donnella has been a guest on Atlanta Live TV and Atlanta Interfaith Broadcaster television stations.

Such outreach initiatives as the Naked Truth Rally, a teen abstinence forum hosted by Debutantes 4 Christ, has also been featured in the *Atlanta Journal Constitution*.

Minister Cranford is retired from the educational system but continues her work as a private consultant, motivational speaker, and minister of the Gospel. She resides in Fayetteville, Georgia, with her beloved husband and best friend, Haywood, her son, Paul, and mother, Maude Brown.

To contact Donnella:
Visit: www.wagohmin.org
Email: wagohmin@aol.com
Mail: P. O. Box 142845
Fayetteville, GA 30214
Phone: 770-460-1369

FROM GOD'S HEART TO YOURS